# Ukulele

*The Ultimate Guide to Mastering Uk*
*30 Minutes or Less!*

# Table of Contents

# Introduction

First and foremost I want to thank you for downloading the book, "Ukulele: The Ultimate Guide to Mastering Ukulele for Beginners in 30 Minutes or Less!"

The ukulele has always been associated with soft, joyful tones and the amazingly captivating state of Hawaii. It is an instrument that perfectly fits together with the schema of a luau by the beach, complete with beautiful Hawaiian dancers with puka necklaces dangling from their necks. Plus, it has always been seen by many people as an instrument that looks like a guitar, but only smaller. But what really is the story of the ukulele? Does it sound like a guitar at all? What are its similarities with the guitar or to the other members of the family of string instruments? And most importantly, how do you play it? These are the questions that will surely be answered by the time you finish reading this book.

In this book you will learn how to serenade and entertain your friends and family with the use of the cute and adorable ukulele. Basically, you will learn the relevant information about the said instrument just like the origin of this instrument, its parts, as well as the basic techniques that you need to learn in order to successfully use the ukulele as accompaniment to any song of your choice such as strumming, plucking, finger positioning to play a chord and more.

Thanks again for downloading this book. I hope you enjoy every page of it! And without further ado, let us begin our musical journey to mastering the ukulele!

# Chapter 1    Meet and Greet with the Ukulele

In the movie entitled *50 First Dates* which starred Adam Sandler and Drew Barrymore, Adam's character played the ukulele for Drew's character during one of their dates. They were sitting by the fire and Adam started to play an original song on his ukulele and serenaded Drew.

If you have seen this movie and remembered this part, it is guaranteed that you swooned over Adam, found his musical gesture sweet, charming and affectionate or made you idolize him and thought you'd try the same thing for your girl during your next night out.

Also, if you have seen this motion picture or if you haven't but you are just a fan of the flowery, sunny and majestic state of Hawaii, you are surely familiar with the string instrument called the *ukulele* – the little guitar with four strings whose actual name most people misspell 99% of the time.

The ukulele (most people misspell it as "ukelele"), as it has been mentioned previously, is a member of the string family or chordophones, together with the likes of the guitar, the violin and the cello. It greatly resembles the guitar when it comes to its physical appearance but the sounds that generates from the ukulele are softer, more festive and gentler than the sounds that a guitar makes, which are more romantic and sharper. Also, the ukulele is much smaller in size compared to a guitar. Another difference between the two is that the ukulele only has 4 strings, while the guitar has 6 strings.

The ukulele, even though it upholds a great connection with the marvelous place of Hawaii, started its trace from mainland Europe. Lutes and guitars were already popular during the 18th century and by the succeeding years people have begun making mini version of these instruments so that sea farers and travelers can bring them aboard the ship with no much hassle. In the Madeira Islands of Portugal for example, people have made the guitar smaller and they propagated an instrument called the *machete* or *machete de braga* which was a descendant of the plucked stringed instrument from Europe and the Middle East. Before it was popularly known as the ukulele, it had first been baptized with several names such as *cavaquinho, braguinha, manchhete* and *cavaco*, just to name a few. This instrument found its way to Hawaii when several Psortuguese immigrants brought this instrument to the land between the years 1878 and 1913. They said that the first original makers of the ukulele were Portuguese settlers by the names of *Manuel Nunes, Augusto Dias* and *Jose do Espirito Santo*. They made more of these little guitars which became a great Hawaiian hit after *King David Kalakaua*, the head of the *Ali'i* or Hawaiian Royal bloodline developed a fondness for this instrument. The Hawaiian royal family commanded the performance of the instrument ever since *Joao Fernandez*, a Portuguese immigrant who was a musical prodigy, played the ukulele in front of the Hawaiian audience for the first time. Since then, the ukulele craze spread like wildfire in the whole of Hawaii and furniture makers converted their business to become ukulele makers instead.

So what is the story behind the name "ukulele"? The term ukulele is a traditional Hawaiian term that means *jumping flea*. The story of how the instrument got its Hawaiian name was more or less lost or altered by time so historians mostly relied on the myths and the legends that tried to explain the etymology of the name. According to one popular legend, the ukulele got its name from an act made by Joao Fernandez. He was so excited to see and reach mainland Hawaii after seeing nothing but sea for four months that he just jumped out of the ship and played folk songs with his little guitar. The natives who saw him play also thought that his fingers were like jumping fleas over the fingerboard and they just started to chant, "Ukulele! Ukulele!"; hence, the *"jumping flea"* connotation.

When the Hawaiian island was sold off to the Americans somewhere in 1915 and 1920, the ukulele was introduced to the American people as well. The ukulele became a hit to American people who wanted to dream about the experience of Hawaii, its majestic beaches and its beautiful ambiance. And soon, the ukulele craze tapped different countries all over the globe until it became a well-loved and well-known instrument.

Today, the ukulele is beginning to gain popularity again, with a lot of internet sites, channels and books offering hundreds of tutorials on how to play it. Celebrities and media personalities are also trying their hand in playing this cutesy little instrument. So, with the help of this book and a little bit of hard work, I can't see why you can't be good with the ukulele as well.

# Chapter 2    Oh Ukulele, You're So Fine

Before you can bust some moves on the ukulele and gain the appreciation and admiration of your colleagues, peers, family members and loved ones by playing this instrument, you must first learn how to choose the perfect ukulele. Choosing the right ukulele or any instrument for that matter is kind of like choosing the right car or the perfect apartment. You have to be meticulous and you have to scrutinize every fine detail so that you can get the worth of your money or investment. It is also important to remember that the music which a musician makes is partly dependent upon the quality of his or her instrument and the harmonious relationship that exists between the musician and the instrument. That is why it is a requisite for you to know your ukulele well because it will become your companion in your musical journey and the key to your musical success.

The first thing to learn about the ukulele is the different parts that make this instrument a whole. The topmost part of the ukulele is called the *head*. This is the part where the tuning adjusters are situated. The *tuning adjusters* are pegs that are used to tune the ukulele. The four tuning adjusters of a ukulele can be turned from left to right or right to left in order to achieve the perfect tune that you are aiming for. The next part is called the *neck* or the *fret board*. It is where the frets are found and it is where you can hold down the strings to play the different chords or notes. The next part is called the *body*. The body of the ukulele, which kind of resembles the torso of a human, is where the sounds resonate. Like that of the body of the guitar, the body of the ukulele has a hole at the center wherein the sounds go into and vibrate through the walls of the body. Then, there is the *saddle* and the *bridge* which supports the strings of the ukulele.

Now that you already know the parts of a ukulele, the next thing to learn is what the parts of the ukulele are made up of. The traditional ukulele is mostly made up of wood but since this instrument has found its way to the hearts of the modern public, there also have been versions that are made out of plastic. Though plastic ukuleles are much more accessible and relatively cheaper compared to traditional ones, the best ukuleles are still those that are made from original wood.

A typical ukulele can be made from Hawaiian koa tree wood, walnut, maple, mahogany, myrtle, Brazilian canary, rosewood, elm, cocobolo, black limba, lacewood or madrone. Choosing the best kind of wood for a ukulele has an impact on the quality of the sound that the ukulele makes. While ukuleles manufactured from Hawaii are made from koa wood, majority of the expert ukulele manufacturers and makers recommend the mahogany as the best type of wood to use because ukuleles made from mahogany wood create soft and mellow tones which is perfect for creating that warm and cozy atmosphere. Mahogany wood also makes a ukulele sound better through time. So, if it's your first time to buy a ukulele and you want something that will surely emit a fine sound, it is recommended that you try out the pieces that are made from mahogany.

As for the strings, most ukuleles use nylon strings. However there are also steal strings for those who are looking for another option other than nylon. The difference between the two types of strings is in the kind of sound that they make. Nylon strings create soft bass sounds while the steal strings create sharp and relatively high pitched sounds. The other materials used in making a ukulele include the adhesives, plastic, paint and steel.

There are also several kinds of ukulele that are available in the market, each with different sizes, different tones and different lengths. There is the *soprano ukulele* which is the most popular, widely used and the tiniest ukulele out of all the other types. It measures 21 inches in length and has 12 to 15 frets which are situated narrowly and tightly together. This kind of ukulele creates the liveliest and the jangliest of sounds. This is not the best ukulele to use for individuals who have big hands though because of the way the frets are situated. Having big hands will make you prone to the possibility of bending the strings out of tune.

There is also the *alto ukulele* or the *concert ukulele* which measures 23 inches long, a little bit longer than the soprano ukulele. This kind of ukulele has 15 to 20 frets which are located slightly farther from each other. Since it is larger in size and the tension on its strings are greater, it creates a fuller and stronger sound. This kind of ukulele is recommended for individuals who have heavy fingers.

If you want a much fuller and bigger sound, you can opt for the *tenor ukulele* which is 26 inches in length and have 15 frets which allow the player to achieve higher pitched notes.

And lastly, there is the *baritone ukulele* which measures 30 inches in length and produces the deepest, crisp and sprightly sound among the four kinds of ukulele. This kind is great for playing the blues because it has 19 frets which allow you to reach a wide range of sounds.

There you have it. Now that you are already knowledgeable about the best materials that are used in making the ukulele, as well as the kinds of ukuleles available to you, you can now choose the perfect ukulele that will suit your taste and the kind of music that you want to create. So next time that you go out and buy a ukulele, make remember these tips and figure out what ukulele is best for you.

# Chapter 3    Do Re Mi Fa So La Ti Tune It Up

The distinction between a master of the ukulele and a mere individual who knows how to play it lies in the ability to tune the instrument. Tuning is a skill that all expert musicians must be knowledgeable in. However, not all musicians can do it. It is an ability that must be independently learned from strumming, fingering and playing the ukulele per se.

Why is it important to be able to learn how to tune the ukulele, or any instrument, properly? The answer is simple. Tuning makes the perfect harmonization between how you want the music to sound and how the music from your ukulele actually sounds possible. If your instrument is in the right tune, then the music that you will make out of your ukulele will sound beautiful and most importantly, right.

For the different kinds of ukuleles, there are also corresponding tuning adjustments. For the soprano ukulele, the strings are tuned to the G C E A or the standard ukulele tuning and A D F# B or the English tuning scale. For the alto ukulele, you follow the G C E A tuning format. For the tenor ukulele, its strings are adjusted to fit the G C E A tuning. And lastly for the baritone ukulele, we follow the D G B E tuning or the baritone ukulele tuning. You can also set you ukulele to the G C E G or slack-key tuning, or to the low A D F# B tuning, popularly known as the Canadian tuning.

You might find yourself confused about the different tuning patterns. You must be wondering, "What are all these letters?" Relax. The letters are not something to be afraid of. They are just simply the representation of the different notes. C refers to "do", D refers to "re", E refers to "mi", F refers to "fa", G refers to "sol", A refers to "la" and B refers to "ti". The standard G C E A tuning pattern means that you have to adjust the strings so that they are in the tune of "sol" for the first string, "do" for the second, "mi" for the third and "la" for the fourth string. The first string is the string nearest to your face when you look down on your ukulele while the fourth string is the farthest from your eyes. This very same principle applies to the other tuning patterns.

One crucial factor in knowing how to tune your ukulele is having knowledge of the perfect pitch for each string. Expert musicians and ukulele players tune their instruments through *manual tuning*. Usually, there are two ways in which you can manually tune your ukulele. That is through piano or through guitar. When using the piano, make sure that the middle C key is in harmony with the sound of the ukulele's second string. Then, try playing the middle E key and see if the sound of your ukulele's third string corresponds with it. Next, play the middle G key of the piano and see if it sounds the same with your ukulele's first string. And lastly, check if your ukulele's fourth string sounds the same with the piano's middle A string. If the tones of that the piano and the ukulele make are alike, then your ukulele is in the right tune.

If you want to use the guitar in tuning your ukulele, you just have to see if the corresponding guitar strings give off the same sound as your ukulele strings. The E string of the guitar on the 5th fret corresponds to the ukulele's A string. The open E string (open string means you don't hold it down or don't press it) of the guitar corresponds to the ukulele's E string. The guitar's B string, held down on the first fret corresponds with the ukulele's C string. And lastly, the E string of the guitar on the 3rd fret corresponds to the G string of the ukulele. If they these guitar strings give off the same sound as your ukulele strings, then your ukulele is tuned to go.

If you don't have the gift of perfect pitch or if you can't seem to learn how to tune your ukulele with the use of either the piano or the guitar no matter what you do, then you have modern technology to thank for. You can opt for the electronic tuner to help you. This device automatically detects the pitch of each string. All you have to is to clip it at the head of the ukulele and then see if the pin on the screen stays pointing at the middle when you strum a chord. If it does, you can say your ukulele is perfectly tuned to go. There are also more high tech variants of the electronic tuner. Some can detect the note that each string makes so you will surely have no hassle in tuning your ukulele.

So remember: tuning will help you make that right and beautiful sound. Never take it for granted because it is the key to creating wonderful music.

# Chapter 4    The G, The F, The E The A B C D

We have already finished the discussion on the preparatory procedures that you need to know before you can learn how to play the ukulele. We have also already discussed the origin of the ukulele and the etymology of its name. We have also finished discussing about the materials that are used in making the ukulele and how to choose the right kind of ukulele for you. And recently, we have finished learning the different techniques in tuning the ukulele so that it will sound perfect and great.

Now, let us progress into the most basic lesson in learning how to play the ukulele and that is learning how to play the chords. The basic major chords are the C, the D, the E, the F, the G, the A and the B. Although the ukulele and the guitar look similar, they don't have the same number of strings. So the way you play chords on the guitar is definitely different on how you play them on the ukulele. It can be said that the ukulele is much easier to play than the guitar because you only have to deal with 4 strings.

For this book, we will focus on the simple and basic chords. The basics are the foundation of more complex chords so it is important to learn them.

There are 7 major chords, two of which (B and E) are not simple to play. The C chord on the ukulele is the easiest chord to play because you only have to hold down one string. To play the *C chord*, all you need to do is press the fourth string on the third fret using your ring finger and voila! You now have the tune of the C chord. The *A chord* is quite easy to play as well. All you need to do is to hold the first string on the second fret using your middle finger and the second string on the first fret using your index finger simultaneously. The finger positioning of the *F chord* is more or less the same with the A chord. The only difference is that playing the F chord doesn't need you to hold down the second string but the third string on the first fret using your index finger. The *D chord* also just consists of holding the first, second and the third string on the second fret simultaneously with your index, middle and ring finger. The *G chord* is quite simple to play too because you just have to remember a triangle in the pattern. To play it, you need to hold down the second string (using your ring finger) and the third string (using your index finger), both on the second fret, simultaneously plus the third string on the third fret using your middle finger. The *E chord* is a bit difficult to play because the points in the neck of the ukulele wherein you have to position your fingers into are quite far apart from each other. To play the E chord, you need to hold the first string on the first fret, the last string on the second fret and the second string on the fourth fret simultaneously. The *B chord* involves pressing all of the four strings. To play this chord, you need to hold the third and last string, both on the second fret, the second string on the third fret and the first string on the fourth fret simultaneously.

Now that we are done with the major chords, let us look into how the minor chords are played. The simplest minor chord that you can play on the ukulele is the *A minor chord.* Like the C major chord, you only have to hold down one string. To play the A minor chord, all you have to do is press the first string on the second fret using your middle finger. The *C minor chord* is also quite simple to play too. All you need to do is to position your fingers on the third fret and then hold down the second, third and the fourth string simultaneously. The *D minor chord* can be played by holding the third string on the first fret, then the first and second string, both on the second fret, simultaneously. To play the *E minor chord* all you need to remember is a diagonal line. You need to press the second string on the fourth fret, the third string on the third fret and then the fourth string on the fourth fret all together. To play the *F minor chord,* all you need to do is simultaneously hold down the first string and the third string, both on the first fret, together with the last string on the third fret. The *G minor chord* can be played by holding down the last string on the first fret, the second string on the second fret and the third string on the third fret simultaneously. And lastly, you can play the *B minor chord* by simultaneously pressing down the second, third and fourth string, all on the second fret, as well as the first string on the fourth fret.

Those are the chords that you need to master so that you can play any song of your choice. They may be difficult to play at first and it might be even harder to remember where to position your fingers in order to play the correct chord but through time, considering that you will persevere and do lots and lots of practice, your brain will get used to it and you will have no difficulty in remembering the chords or trying to figure out where your fingers should be. If you train and practice hard enough, you can even do these things with your eyes closed.

# Chapter 5    Strum It Like You Mean It

Being an expert with the ukulele does not only stop at knowing where to position your fingers on the neck or fret board in order to make the sound of the different chords. You also need to learn how to properly strum the strings in order to make a melody that is pleasant to the ear and not just a cacophonous sound.

Strumming the strings of the ukulele creates the rhythm and the beat which, in order to be effective, needs a steady and consistent strumming pattern. To make strumming more convenient and effective, you must first know the strumming hand position. First, hold your ukulele against your chest without applying too much pressure on it. Just make yourself comfortable and relax. Then, make sure that you form your strumming hand into a loose fist and let your thumb support the finger that you want to use for strumming. Usually, ukulele players use their index finger and their thumb to make their strumming more concise and steady. Also, do not strum the strings near the bridge of the ukulele for this will generate tiny sounds. It is advisable to strum near the part where the neck of the ukulele meets the body.

Strumming patterns usually involve up and down motions and knowing what part of your finger the strings will hit while doing these movements will have an impact on the sound that you will create. When you strum down, make sure that your nail hits the strings. When you strum up, let the strings hit the tip of your finger. You might want to also use your wrist when strumming rather than moving your whole arm. This will prevent your hand from being tired and numb instantly.

In strumming the ukulele, there are several strumming techniques that are suitable for beginners. The simplest strumming pattern which is composed of just downward strumming movements can be considered as the foundation of the other patterns. Count from 1 to 4 as you strum the strings in a downward motion and try to align the beat of the song with your strumming. Remember: you don't have to strum up, just down. Master this and later you can add upward strums in between each downward strumming.

The next strumming pattern is already composed of upward and downward strumming. Strum the strings of the ukulele down then up then down and up again. Basically, it is just the first strumming pattern but with the addition of the upward strumming motion. The pattern goes like this: up, down, up and down. As you strum, try to practice changing chords as well. Switch the chords on the first beat of the pattern.

The third strumming pattern that you should try is a combination of the first and second pattern. Strum your strings starting with a downward strum then another downward strum, and then upward strum, back to downward strum. This pattern basically goes like this: down, down, up and down, down, up and down.

The next strumming pattern is just a rearrangement of the third strumming pattern. Instead of two consecutive downward strums, you strum downwards then upwards then downwards and downwards again. The pattern goes like this: down, up, down and down.

The last strumming pattern that you can try is the reverse of the third pattern. You still have to start with the pattern of down, down, up. But during the second loop, you start with the upward strumming instead of the downward. This is how the pattern works: down, down, up and up then down and up.

As you practice on these patterns, strumming will become more natural for you and you don't have to count to get the sequence right anymore. Once you become an expert in strumming, all you have to do is listen to the beat and rhythm of the song and just go with it.

Aside from strumming the strings of the ukulele, you can also try to use the *finger picking or plucking technique*. In this technique, you are going to use your thumb, which will pluck the 3rd and 4th string; the middle finger, which will pluck the 1st string; and the index finger which will pluck the 2nd string. In contrast to the strumming technique which needs you to hit the strings together at once, plucking or finger picking will need you to "pick" on each string and let them individually make a sound. To help you in making your picking hand stable, you can use your pinky as support. Finger picking or plucking is considered as considered as a more advanced technique than strumming because it needs speed, accuracy and coordination between the fingers that are holding the strings and the fingers that are plucking the strings to make them create a sound. Before trying on this technique, be sure to learn how to properly strum first.

Sometimes, strumming and finger picking can lead to a disaster and the snapping of your strings into two, especially if you turned the tuning adjusters too tight or if you applied to much pressure on the strings. If this happens to your ukulele, don't worry. You don't have to buy a new one or throw your instrument away. You just have to replace the strings and insert new ones. In order to remove the strings, you just simply loosen the tuning adjusters and unwind the strings. Then, push the loose strings through the holes of the bridge. Once this is done, you can either cut the knot at the end of the string or untie it. To insert new strings, first you have to slide the string into the hole of the bridge and then make a knot. Once this is done, wrap the string around the tuning adjusters. Do not forget to apply your knowledge on tuning after replacing your strings.

Just like tuning and learning the basic chords used to play the ukulele, strumming and plucking needs practice too. So, never forget to practice and practice until you finally succeed.

# Chapter 6     What's The Song?

Now that you already know the techniques and tricks in playing your ukulele, you can now play a song of your choice. For this book, you will be taught simple songs that you can use in order to practice playing your ukulele to. These songs may be simple folk or nursery songs but they are great for practice purposes.

Twinkle, Twinkle Little Star is a great starter song if you want to apply your knowledge on the basic techniques in playing the ukulele. This song involves a simple quarter rhythm and a lot of open strings. The chords for this song are these: C F C F C G C C G C G C G C G then repeat from the top.

Another song that is easy to try in the ukulele is London Bridge Is Falling Down. The chords that you need to know in order to play this song are just the C chord, the G chord and the C chord. Just keep repeating this pattern until the end of the song. And since the song entitled Mary Had A Little Lamb has the same tune as London Bridge, these two songs also share the same chord progression.

If you want to play a more modern song, you can try the song called Hey Soul Sister by the band called Train. This song is so easy to play for it only utilizes four chords and those are G Am F and C.

The popular song entitled Thinking Out Loud by Ed Sheeran is pretty easy to play on the ukulele as well. The chords that you need for this song are C Am F G and Dm.

If you are a fan of Disney's Frozen and can't stop singing Do You Wanna Build A Snowman, why don't you accompany your singing voice with the tune of the ukulele? This song only needs the chords C G Am F and E in order to successfully play it.

Okay. Once you learn and master these songs on the ukulele, you can progress into much more complex songs. But before you play those tunes, why don't you get started with these and have fun while you are at it? Enjoy!

# Conclusion

Thank you again for downloading this book! It has been a great joy to share to you the basic knowledge, tips and tricks that will greatly help you in becoming a master of the ukulele.

I hope this book was able to help you to understand and get to know the instrument better. Often times, the ukulele is deemed inferior to the guitar and to the other string instruments. But what most people don't realize is that this small and tiny instrument also have what it takes to take part in making an orchestra or a band sound greater and more beautiful. In short, the ukulele is the perfect example of small but terrible. I also hope that through reading this book, you were able to understand the basic concepts and techniques used in playing the ukulele. They were practically very easy to follow and try. I hope you were encouraged to practice and learn more about the ukulele and use the knowledge that you were able to acquire from this book as a stepping stone into making yourself an expert in the ukulele.

The next step upon successful completion of this book is to of course practice and apply what you have learned. Without practice, the skills that you learned from this book will never be enhanced and cultivate. Try tuning your ukulele on your own without the help of an electronic device. Try to play the songs that were mention in the last chapter. Try to replace your strings without any help or guide. Try the different strumming patterns. Try and try and practice until you become an expert. May you also pass on to others your skills and knowledge about the ukulele so that you can inspire others to learn and love this instrument as much as this book has encouraged and inspired you to pick that ukulele up and learn it. Remember as well to always practice and practice no matter how good you become for a great musician always tries to become the better version of him or her. He or she never stops learning.

Finally, if you enjoyed this book, please take the time to share your thoughts and post a review on Amazon. It'd be greatly appreciated!

Thank you and good luck!

# Bonus Chapter: Beginner Guitar Techniques 101 and Terminology

All the guitars, despite their different artistic appearance, define specific characteristics that make them unique.

The following sections consist of the description of different parts of the guitar and their functions, the proper way of holding the instrument, and some explanations for the special sounds produced.

The main flavors on the guitar menu are acoustic and electric. The electric guitar is richer than the acoustic one on a hardware point of view since it has more components and doohickeys. However, it is a general agreement among guitar makers that the assembling of an acoustic guitar in terms of components and functionality is more complex than that of electric guitars, the same reason why an acoustic guitar is more expensive.

The illustration below shows the different parts of the guitar, both acoustic and electric, followed by the descriptions and functions.

***Back (acoustic only):*** The body part holding the sides in place comprising of two or three wood pieces.

***Bar (electric only):***A metal rod with an attachment to the bridge to provide a variation of the string tension by back and forth tilting of the bridge.

***Body:*** The box with a provision of an anchor to the neck and bridge and also responsible for the creation of the right hand playing surface. On an acoustic guitar, the body comprises of an amplifying sound chamber for the provision of the guitar tone. On an electric guitar, it consists of the bridge assembly for electronics and housing.

***Bridge:*** The wooden (acoustic) or metal (electric) plate that provides an anchor for the body strings.

***End pin:*** A metal post providing a connection to strap's rear ends.

***Fingerboard:*** A metal post providing a connection to strap's rear ends.

**Headstock:** The section holding the tuning machines and also a provision for a place for the display of the manufacturer's logo.

**Neck:** The long and club-like wooden piece connecting the body to the headstock.

**Nut:** A synthetic substance preventing the vibration of the strings beyond the neck.

**Output jack (electric only):** A point of insertion for the cord connecting the guitar to other electronic devices such as an amplifier.

**Pickup selector (electric only):** A switch that gives a determination of the currently active pickups.

**Pickups (electric only):** Bar-like magnets responsible for the electrical current creation, for musical sound conversion by the amplifier.

**Sides (acoustic only):** A curved separate wooden piece on the body joining the top to the back.

**Strap pin:** A post of metal connecting the front or top, strap end.

**Strings:** The nylon or six metal wires responsible for the production of the guitar notes.

**Top:** The guitar's face, a sounding board on an acoustic and a decorative cap on an electric.

**Tuning machines:** Some geared mechanisms for raising and lowering the string's tension.

**Volume and tone controls (electric only):** Knobs that help in manipulatingthe guitar's sound like treble and bass frequencies.

After a brief description of the various parts of the guitar, it should interest you on how these parts synchronize and produce an elegant sound. This information would help you understand how and why the guitar produces such an intuitive sound. Not to be confused, sound production comes from the guitar but the music comes from its user.

It is common for a musical instrument to have a pattern-like motion producing musical sound, tone or pitch. When it sums down to the guitar, the vibrating string emits the sound. Strings brought to a certain level of tension that if the motion is added, a delightful sound is emitted.

The creation of music by a guitar requires the coordination of two hands. Dealing with a guitar is different from dealing with other instruments. The half step seems to be the smallest musical scale interval. On the guitar, the frets are a representation of the half steps. The half steps up or down movement on a guitar is the left-hand movement between frets. The movement can either be higher or lower; adjacent to the neck. The production of distinct tones on a guitar comes from its vibrating strings. The problem does not lie in an acoustic guitar since it has amplification in hollow sound form. The sound boost is from the hollow sound chamber.

An acoustic sound is not present on an electric guitar. The creation of electric tones by an electric instrument comes from electronic means. The sound source is still the vibrating string, but the vibration audibility is not based on a hollow wood chamber.

The production of sound by a guitar is either through the amplification of string vibrations acoustically or electronically. The acoustic means passes sound waves via a hollow chamber. The electric means is by the amplification and production of an output sound via a speaker. The stated terms sum up the physical process. Your control of the produced pitches is a determination of the different production of guitar sounds. The change in the pitches is as a result of the left-hand fretting. The right-hand motion causes sound production, rhythm determination, tempo and feel of the pitches. The combination of the left and right-hand motion is a magic spell; guitar music

25940660R00016

Printed in Great Britain
by Amazon